Who's Hiding?

Written by Vicky Shiotsu
Illustrated by Paul Lopez

Who's slithering?
Take a peek.
Someone's playing
hide-and-seek!

2

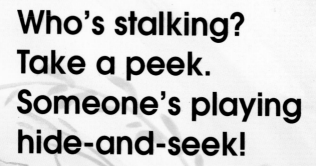

Who's stalking?
Take a peek.
Someone's playing
hide-and-seek!

Who's gliding?
Take a peek.
Someone's playing
hide-and-seek!

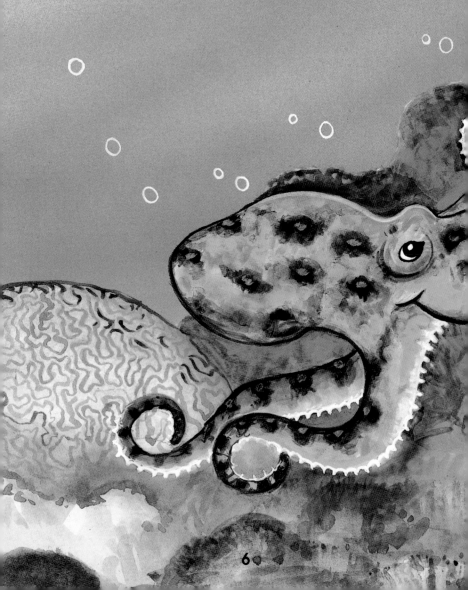

Who's climbing?
Take a peek.
Someone's playing
hide-and-seek!

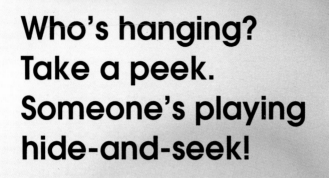

Who's hanging?
Take a peek.
Someone's playing
hide-and-seek!

Who's fluttering?
Take a peek.
Someone's playing
hide-and-seek!

Who's burrowing?
Take a peek.
Someone's playing
hide-and-seek!

chameleor

sloth

tiger

butterfl

squirrel

snake

octopus